This guide is dedicated to my fellow unapologetically
authentic creative entrepreneurs.

You're a star bitch - shine like one!

Your Business, Your Buzz:

A NO-B.S. GUIDE TO PLANNING 12 MONTHS OF CONTENT FOR YOUR CREATIVE BUSINESS

(without selling your soul)

MEGS THOMPSON

INTUITIVE WRITING COACH, WORD-TWERKING
BOOK-DOULA, GHOSTWRITER, EDITOR & PUBLISHER

Cover, Book Design & Layout by megswrites llc
www.megswrites.com

in omnia paratus publishing llc
www.inomniaparatuspublishing.com

CONGRATULATIONS!
Well done! F*ck Yea!

Whether you're already a successful small business owner looking to reclaim your time & stop dreading the content planning process, or a self-employed hopeful still dreaming about birthing your own business & overwhelmed with the insane number of tasks you need to tackle - I've got you!

You might be wondering,

"What qualifies you to coach me on planning content for my business?"

I'm glad you asked!

I'm Megs.

I'm an intuitive writing coach, word-twerking book-doula, ghostwriter, editor & publisher who has spent countless days brainstorming, drafting, outlining, mapping & creating mountains of authentic content for my own businesses - not to mention the hours I've spent helping my clients & colleagues to do the same.

No matter what your business is, whether it's products, services, or something else entirely, coming up with unique, creative posts, reels, stories, polls (& whatever else there is now) can be exhausting & downright frustrating AF. But, it doesn't have to be.

In this quick guide, I've put together the exact steps that I use personally to:

- brainstorm amazing content ideas that speak to YOUR ideal audience!
- map out a content plan that fits YOUR style!
- ditch the stress, headaches & dread associated with content planning!
- rest easy, knowing you're a badass boss & your content shows it!

Ready? Let's do this!

- megs

Step 1: The Braindump

Let's start with the basics to make sure we're all on the same page.

What is content? What does it do? Why does it even matter?!

GREAT content:

- connects authentically with YOUR ideal clients
- answers YOUR ideal clients' questions
- shows off YOU & YOUR brand
- provides value to YOUR audience
- highlights YOUR zone of genius

Now that we've got *that* out of the way, the first step to planning your content is figuring out what YOUR zone of genius is & how YOU can provide value to YOUR ideal audience.

Which brings us to Step 1: The Braindump

For those unfamiliar with the magic of a Braindump, this is basically a quick exercise to get all of the thoughts you have regarding a certain topic or question, out of your head & onto the page.

For this Braindump, we'll be focusing on two primary questions:

- What services do you offer?
- What are your areas of expertise?

Some of your answers to these questions will go on to become your "Monthly Themes" for your new content plan. Meaning you really only need to have 12 things listed, to set yourself up for an ENTIRE YEAR of great content!

On the next page, I've included a few examples of Braindumps to help you get started. When you're ready, use the pages provided to create a dump or two of your own.

Sample Braindumps

As a Relationship Coach, my services and areas of expertise include...

- Setting Healthy Boundaries
- Self Awareness & Reflection
- Communication Skills
- Empathetic Listening
- Goal Setting

As an Interior Designer, my services and areas of expertise include...

- Attention to Detail
- Color Theory
- Spatial Skills
- Time Management
- Design Trends

As a Life Coach, my services and areas of expertise include...

- Effective Communication
- Probing Questions
- Observation Skills
- Empathetic Listening
- Active Listening

What services do you offer?

What are your areas of expertise?

Step 2: The Right Questions

WooHoo! Step 1 - Done!

Feels good, right?!

Alright, now that you've got a TON of notes showcasing your amazingly unique services and areas of expertise, choose 12 of those that you want to focus on this year.

Go ahead and highlight them however you'd like on the last page, as well as jotting them down on the following calendar pages as the "Monthly Theme."

The next step involves digging deeper into each of these themes in a way that ensures you're addressing the ACTUAL questions, concerns, and hesitations that YOUR ideal clients have.

This step is the longest of the content planning process, but worthwhile because it's part market research as well, and helps to improve the understanding you have of your ideal audience.

Step 2: The Right Questions

For each of your new Monthly Themes, list 12-16 questions your ideal clients have related to that specific service or area of expertise.

These questions can be about the problems your audience is seeking to resolve, common misconceptions regarding your service/industry, or common hesitations your ideal clients have when it comes to investing in your services.

Each of these questions will become a topic for your new content plan.

Meaning you only need to have 12-16 questions for each theme, to set yourself up for an ENTIRE YEAR of great content!

You may be wondering,

"Where do I find these magic questions?!"

One of the quickest (and easiest) ways is by crowdsourcing. You can do this by making a post on social media, either your own pages/accounts or within any of the countless Facebook Groups filled with YOUR ideal clients.

Personally, I like to keep these posts short, sweet & straight to the point.

*"What questions would you love to ask a professional *****?"*

*"What's your biggest hesitation when it comes to investing in *****?"*

*"What's one question you're dying to ask a *****?"*

On the next page, I've included a few examples of The Right Questions for a few positions, to help you get started. When you're ready, use the pages provided to create your own lists.

Sample Questions

<u>*Monthly Theme 1: Setting Healthy Boundaries*</u>

- *What are healthy boundaries?*
- *What are unhealthy boundaries?*
- *How do I set healthy boundaries with friends?*
- *How do I set healthy boundaries with family?*
- *How do I set healthy boundaries at work?*
- *How do I set healthy boundaries with myself?*
- *Why are healthy boundaries important?*
- *How do I know if my boundaries are healthy?*
- *What are examples of healthy boundaries?*

<u>*Monthly Theme 2: Goal Setting*</u>

- *Why is goal setting important?*
- *What kind of goals should I be setting?*
- *How do I decide on what goals to set for myself?*
- *How do I hold myself accountable to my goals?*
- *What are some tips for successful goal setting?*
- *What are some tools for successful goal setting?*
- *Is there a process for goal setting?*
- *Should I share my goals with others?*
- *How should I reward myself when I achieve a goal?*

Monthly Theme 1

Monthly Theme 2

Monthly Theme 3

Monthly Theme 4

Monthly Theme 5

Monthly Theme 6

Monthly Theme 7

Monthly Theme 8

Monthly Theme 9

Monthly Theme 10

Monthly Theme 11

Monthly Theme 12

Step 3: The Right Mix

WooHoo! Step 2 - Done!

You're SO CLOSE!

You've got 12 AMAZING Monthly Themes, as well as 12-16 SPECIFIC questions that are going to connect with YOUR ideal audience, and FILL your inbox with requests for more!

It's time to put it all together, and create a content plan that works FOR YOU!

This is where you get to decide HOW you want to communicate with YOUR ideal audience.

Step 3: The Right Mix

The remaining pages are dedicated to better fleshing out each month of your new content plan. Each month has two pages, the first is a planning page, the second is a calendar for visualization. These pages are set up with enough space to plan 2 blog posts, 2 email messages, and 12 social media posts per month.

This works out to a new blog post or email message each week (rotating), and 3 social media posts weekly.

Using the specific questions you created in Step 2, you'll want to decide which you want to address using blog posts, which are better suited for an email message, and which can be tackled best with a social media post.

Once you've decided which topics you'll tackle with which forms of content, you can get to work writing the copy for each of these unique pieces.

I've also provided a sample calendar for reference.

How you choose to schedule your content is completely up to you.

Many of my clients opt to start with the following schedule:

- Social media posts on Monday, Wednesday, and Friday
- Blog posts or email messages on Tuesday or Thursday

That leaves only 1 day each week (if you're taking the weekends off) to post something spontaneous & off the cuff.

This is a great time to show off your fur-kids, office view, or favorite quote! Anything that resonates with your audience, relates to your business/brand, and encourages engagement.

Once you've gotten a feel for your audience, and their habits, you can adjust as needed to ensure you're posting your content on dates/times that fit your audience's schedule & provide them with the type of content that resonates most with them.

The best part is that once you've completed this plan, you can easily repurpose content in the future, making tweaks & changes as needed to ensure information is accurate and relevant.

Happy Planning!

MONTHLY PLANNING PAGES

Sample Monthly Calendar

Monthly Theme:

Setting Healthy Boundaries

Blog Posts:

Why are healthy boundaries important?

How do I know if my boundaries are healthy or unhealthy?

Emails:

What are some examples of healthy boundaries?

What are some examples of unhealthy boundaries?

Social Media Posts:

How to set healthy boundaries with friends

How to set healthy boundaries with family

How to set healthy boundaries at work

How to set healthy boundaries with my spouse/partner

How to set healthy boundaries with myself

How do healthy boundaries make me feel

Personal story about unhealthy boundaries

Personal story about healthy boundaries

Engagement Post about setting healthy boundaries

Humorous Post about setting healthy boundaries

Poll Post about setting healthy boundaries

Free Resource Post about setting healthy boundaries

Sample Monthly Calendar

Mon	Tue	Wed	Thu	Fri	Sat	Sun
Social Media Post	Blog	Social Media Post		Social Media Post		
Social Media Post		Social Media Post	Email	Social Media Post		
Social Media Post	Blog	Social Media Post		Social Media Post		
Social Media Post		Social Media Post	Email	Social Media Post		

January

Monthly Theme:

_____

Blog Posts:

_____

_____

Emails:

_____

_____

Social Media Posts:

_____

_____

_____

_____

_____

_____

_____

_____

_____

_____

January

Sun				
Sat				
Fri				
Thu				
Wed				
Tue				
Mon				

February

Monthly Theme:

_____

Blog Posts:

_____

_____

Emails:

_____

_____

Social Media Posts:

_____

_____

_____

_____

_____

_____

_____

_____

_____

_____

February

Sun				
Sat				
Fri				
Thu				
Wed				
Tue				
Mon				

March

Monthly Theme:

_____

Blog Posts:

_____

_____

Emails:

_____

_____

Social Media Posts:

_____

_____

_____

_____

_____

_____

_____

_____

_____

_____

March

Sun				
Sat				
Fri				
Thu				
Wed				
Tue				
Mon				

April

Monthly Theme:

_____

Blog Posts:

_____

_____

Emails:

_____

_____

Social Media Posts:

_____

_____

_____

_____

_____

_____

_____

_____

_____

_____

April

	Sun	Sat	Fri	Thu	Wed	Tue	Mon

May

Monthly Theme:

_____

Blog Posts:

_____

_____

Emails:

_____

_____

Social Media Posts:

_____

_____

_____

_____

_____

_____

_____

_____

_____

May

Sun				
Sat				
Fri				
Thu				
Wed				
Tue				
Mon				

June

Monthly Theme:

_____

Blog Posts:

_____

_____

Emails:

_____

_____

Social Media Posts:

_____

_____

_____

_____

_____

_____

_____

_____

_____

_____

June

Sun	Sat	Fri	Thu	Wed	Tue	Mon

July

Monthly Theme:

_____

Blog Posts:

_____

_____

Emails:

_____

_____

Social Media Posts:

_____

_____

_____

_____

_____

_____

_____

_____

_____

_____

July

Sun				
Sat				
Fri				
Thu				
Wed				
Tue				
Mon				

August

Monthly Theme:

_____

Blog Posts:

_____

_____

Emails:

_____

_____

Social Media Posts:

_____

_____

_____

_____

_____

_____

_____

_____

_____

_____

August

Sun				
Sat				
Fri				
Thu				
Wed				
Tue				
Mon				

September

Monthly Theme:

_____

Blog Posts:

_____

_____

Emails:

_____

_____

Social Media Posts:

_____

_____

_____

_____

_____

_____

_____

_____

_____

_____

September

Sun				
Sat				
Fri				
Thu				
Wed				
Tue				
Mon				

October

Monthly Theme:

_____

Blog Posts:

_____

_____

Emails:

_____

_____

Social Media Posts:

_____

_____

_____

_____

_____

_____

_____

_____

_____

_____

October

Sun				
Sat				
Fri				
Thu				
Wed				
Tue				
Mon				

November

Monthly Theme:

_____

Blog Posts:

_____

_____

Emails:

_____

_____

Social Media Posts:

_____

_____

_____

_____

_____

_____

_____

_____

_____

November

Sun				
Sat				
Fri				
Thu				
Wed				
Tue				
Mon				

December

Monthly Theme:

_____

Blog Posts:

_____

_____

Emails:

_____

_____

Social Media Posts:

_____

_____

_____

_____

_____

_____

_____

_____

_____

_____

December

Sun				
Sat				
Fri				
Thu				
Wed				
Tue				
Mon				

BAM!
You did it!

insert virtual high five here

All that's left now is to start writing blogs, emails & social media posts for the topics you've outlined & of course, posting them online to engage with your dream clients.

As with anything in life, consistency is key, but so is having fun.

A word to the wise, when you're sitting down to create the pieces of content you've outlined in this workbook, have fun with it! Your audience can tell when you're phoning it in or writing something because you feel like you *have to*.

Your dream clients are going to be drawn to you like flies on shit when they can tell you love what you're doing & can't wait to share your unique brand of magic & expertise with them.

www.ingramcontent.com/pod-product-compliance
Lightning Source LLC
Chambersburg PA
CBHW051333120626
46547CB00016B/2521